#Rip This Book

Create and destroy journal packed with creative activities to draw, doodle, paint, stick, smudge, collage and inspire creativity.

#RIP THIS BOOK

WE LOVE TO SEE YOUR CREATIONS!

PLEASE SHARE YOUR COMPLETED PAGES WITH US ON

INSTAGRAM @ DottyDoodle_s
TIKTOK   @ Dotty.Doodles

Copyright © 2022 Dotty Doodles ISBN 978-1-7397195-3-1
All rights reserved. This book or any portion thereof may not be reproduced or used in any manner whatsoever without the express written permission of the publisher except for the use of brief quotations in a book review.

WWW.DOTTYDOODLES.COM

⚠ WARNING

COMPLETING THIS BOOK WILL BE MESSY.
THE BOOK WILL GET RUINED ON PURPOSE.
MATERIALS WILL BLEED THROUGH THE PAGE.
YOU WILL NEED TO PATCH IT UP WITH EXTRA PAPER, TAPE AND TLC.
THIS BOOK WILL BEAR THE SCARS OF YOUR CREATIVE EXPERIMENTS.
IT WILL BE BRUISED BATTERED AND WILL NEVER LOOK PRISTINE AND NEW EVER AGAIN

ARE YOU READY TO GET STARTED?

DATE STARTED

DATE FINISHED

STEP BACK IN TIME

REMEMBER THOSE DAYS IN PRESCHOOL WHEN ART WAS ALL ABOUT HAVING FUN, TRYING OUT NEW TEXTURES, PROCESSES AND MATERIALS...... AND GETTING REALLY MESSY IN THE PROCESS? STRIVING FOR A PERFECT END RESULT WAS NEVER THE GOAL...... IT WAS ALL ABOUT EXPERIMENTING, HAVING FUN AND THE FREEDOM TO EXPLORE NEW WAYS TO BE CREATIVE.

Do you wish you could go back there?

WELCOME TO RIP THIS BOOK!

SOMEWHERE ALONG THE WAY EVERYTHING CHANGED AND ART BECAME SOMETHING TO BE JUDGED AND GRADED.....
CREATIVE SPARKS GOT SQUASHED. CRUSHED BY THE PRESSURE TO PRODUCE "PROPER" ART THAT MET CERTAIN CRITERIA.
THE FOCUS WAS ON PERFECTING THE END RESULT —SUCKING ALL THE JOY OUT OF THE CREATIVE PROCESS.

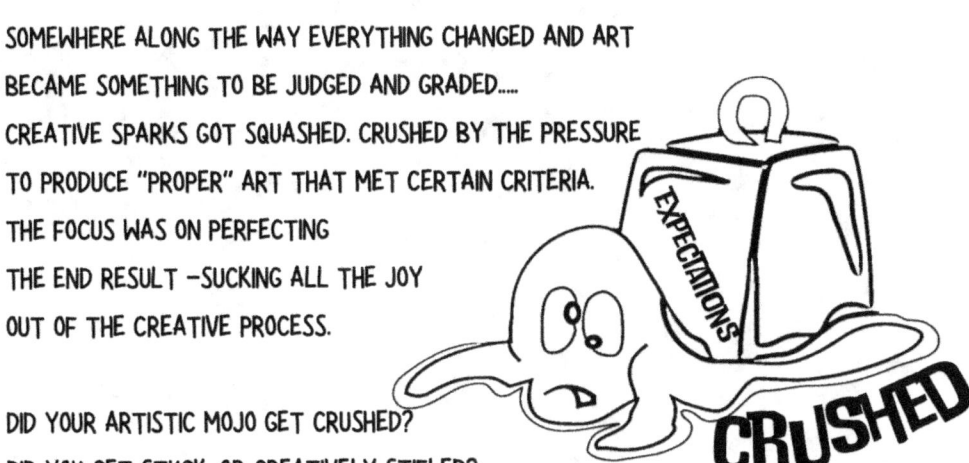

DID YOUR ARTISTIC MOJO GET CRUSHED?
DID YOU GET STUCK, OR CREATIVELY STIFLED?

THIS IS WHERE WE FIGHT BACK!

THIS BOOK IS YOUR INVITATION TO EMBRACE THE MESSY, FUN, JUVENILE ART YOU USED TO LOVE.

YOU AND THIS BOOK ARE GOING ON A JOURNEY OF CREATIVITY RIGHT BACK TO THOSE FINGER PAINTING DAYS IN PRESCHOOL WHERE YOU DID LEAF RUBBINGS AND BUTTERFLY PICTURES AND CAME HOME COVERED IN PAINT GLUE AND GLITTER.

LET'S GO BACK TO YOUR CREATIVE ROOTS AND FALL IN LOVE WITH YOUR ARTY CRAFT SIDE ALL OVER AGAIN.

GET READY TO SPRINKLE, SMUDGE, SMEAR AND SCRATCH YOUR CREATIVE GLITTER ALL OVER THE PAGES OF THIS BOOK.

ARE YOU READY?
LET'S DIVE STRAIGHT IN AND GET STARTED!

BEGINNING CAN BE THE HARDEST PART – SO DON'T OVERTHINK IT – JUST GET GOING.
START ANYWHERE.
DON'T WORRY ABOUT FAILING OR MAKING MISTAKES.
YOU DON'T EVEN HAVE TO SHOW ANYONE THE END RESULT.

THE RULES

- DON'T OVERTHINK
- DO YOUR OWN THING
- DON'T STRIVE FOR PERFECTION — THE PROCESS IS MORE IMPORTANT THAN THE END RESULT
- CHOOSE YOUR OWN WAY
- EXPERIMENT — TRY NEW THINGS
- DON'T PLAY IT SAFE
- don't be afraid to get messy
- EMBRACE YOUR MISTAKES — BE PERFECTLY IMPERFECT!
- HAVE FUN

FOLLOW THE RULES OR DON'T FOLLOW THE RULES — IT'S UP TO YOU

ME! ME! ME!

WRITE YOUR NAME OVER AND OVER IN DIFFERENT STYLES. SIGN YOUR AUTOGRAPH, WRITE IT BIG, WRITE IT SMALL, WRITE BACKWARDS OR IN BUBBLE WRITING.....

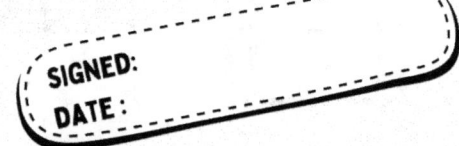

hey baby

LET'S GROW TOGETHER

DOCUMENT HOW YOUR JOURNAL
GROWS DURING THE CREATIVE PROCESS

MEASURE THE THICKNESS OF YOUR BOOK

START ....

MID POINT ....

FINISH...

DOCUMENT BEFORE AND AFTER PICTURES HERE

BEFORE

AFTER

SIGNED:
DATE :

GOALS FOR THIS BOOK

SIGNED:
DATE :

SET YOUR INTENTIONS FOR USING THIS BOOK

TURN ON THE LIGHT

**L
I
G
H
T**

THERE IS SOMETHING I NEED TO SAY

SIGNED:
DATE:

create a page

SIGNED:
DATE:

of TRIANGLES

kiss my.... page

COLLECT KISSES ON THIS PAGE

SIGNED:
DATE :

ADVERTISE THIS PAGE

SIGNED:
DATE:

CREATE BUNTING
AND HANG IT HERE

SIGNED:
DATE:

DESIGN AND CUT OUT THE BUNTING FLAGS AND USE IT TO DECORATE THE PREVIOUS PAGE

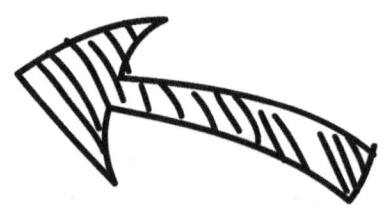

this page is deliberately blank so you can cut out the
flags on the opposite side

DELETE THIS PAGE

SIGNED:
DATE:

SIGNED:
DATE :

PAINT THIS PAGE USING YOUR FINGERS

COLLECT TOGETHER STICKY THINGS YOU WOULD **NOT** EXPECT TO SEE ON A PAGE

SIGNED:
DATE:

TO INFINITY........∞

create a never ending line

SIGNED:
DATE :

FLYING OFF

THE PAGE

SNIP SNIP

CUT THE PAGES IN AN ARTFUL WAY

SIGNED:
DATE:

FREESTYLE
THIS PAGE

SIGNED:
DATE:

DOODLE THE WHOLE PAGE

SIGNED:
DATE:

SIGNED:
DATE :

NO PEEPING

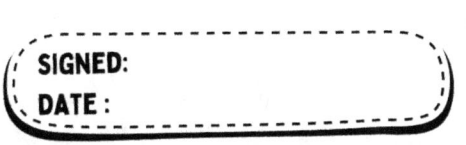

DROP, SPRAY, TRICKLE OR DRIP

SOMETHING ON THIS PAGE

SIGNED:
DATE :

TOTALLY RANDOM

PASTE RANDOM TUFF ALL VER THIS PAGE

SIGNED:
DATE:

SIGNED:
DATE:

CREATE A SHINY PAGE

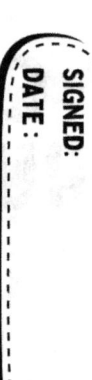

SIGNED:
DATE:

CREATE RUBBINGS WITH A CRAYON

2 **1** **3**

SIGNED:
DATE :

FOLD OR CREASE THIS PAGE IN A CREATIVE WAY

SIGNED:
DATE :

DRAW, STICK, DOODLE OR COLLAGE THE LETTER YOUR NAME STARTS WITH

SIGNED:
DATE :

SIGNED:
DATE:

CREATE A SECRET CODE

make a symbol for each letter of the alphabet to write your secret messages

A	B
C	D	E	F
G	H	I	J
K	L	M	N
O	P	Q	R
S	T	U	V
W	X	Y	Z

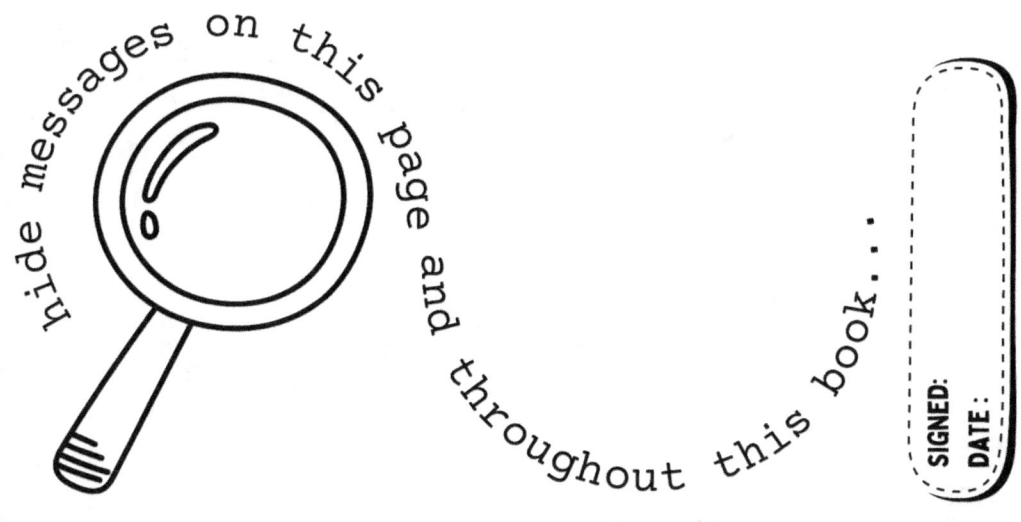

SIGNED:
DATE :

Make This Page Look Old

REPURPOSE JUNK MAIL INTO
ART

SIGNED:
DATE :

SIGNED:
DATE :

CAPPTURED

WHAT'S IN THE WEB?

RIP THIS PAGE

SIGNED:
DATE:

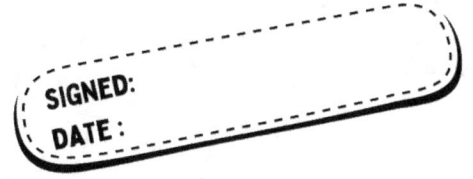

DO NOT LEAVE THIS PAGE BLANK

FIND A WAY TO TIE SOMETHING TO THIS PAGE

NEON
MAKE A PAGE THAT IS SUPER BRIGHT

SIGNED:
DATE:

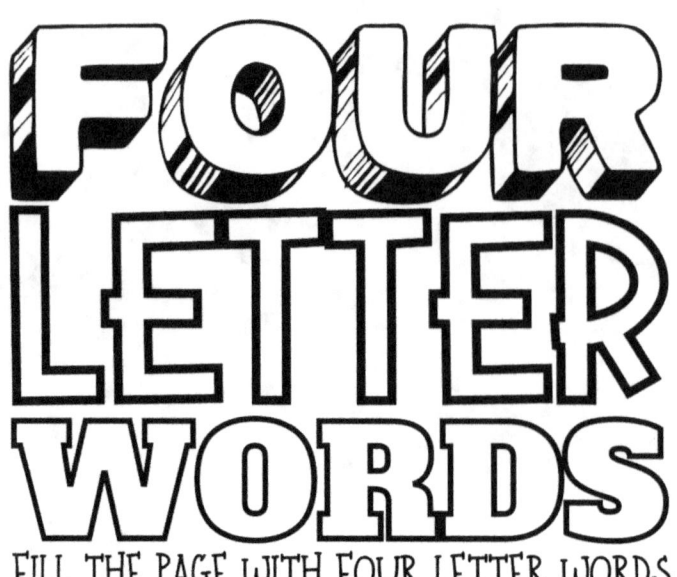
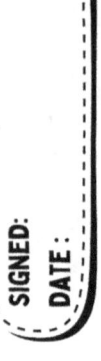

FILL THE PAGE WITH FOUR LETTER WORDS

SDRAWKCAB

CREATE A PAGE WITH A BACKWARDS THEME

SIGNED:
DATE:

SIGNED:
DATE:

WITH STRING

SIGNED:
DATE:

DECORATE THIS PAGE WITH STICKERS

SIGNED:
DATE :

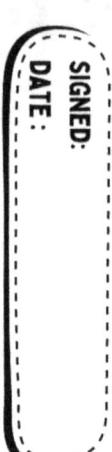

SIGNED:
DATE :

COLLECT NUMBERS

ON THIS PAGE

SIGNED:
DATE :

CREATE A PRICKLY PAGE
OUCH!

SIGNED:
DATE:

SIGNED:
DATE :

my life in stains

RUB, SMEAR, DRIP, SMUDGE OR SPLATTER
DOCUMENT A DAY IN YOUR LIFE IN STAINS

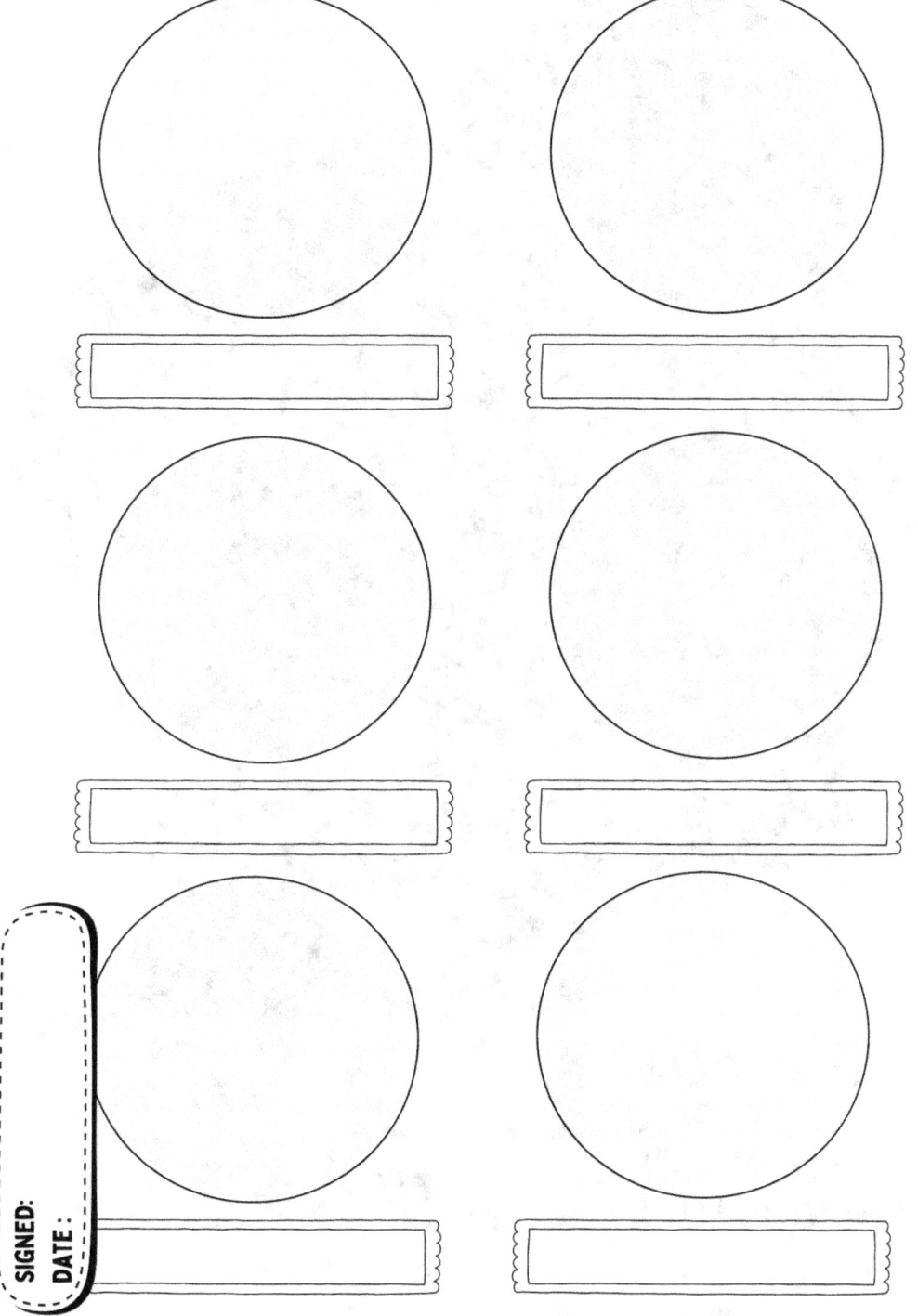

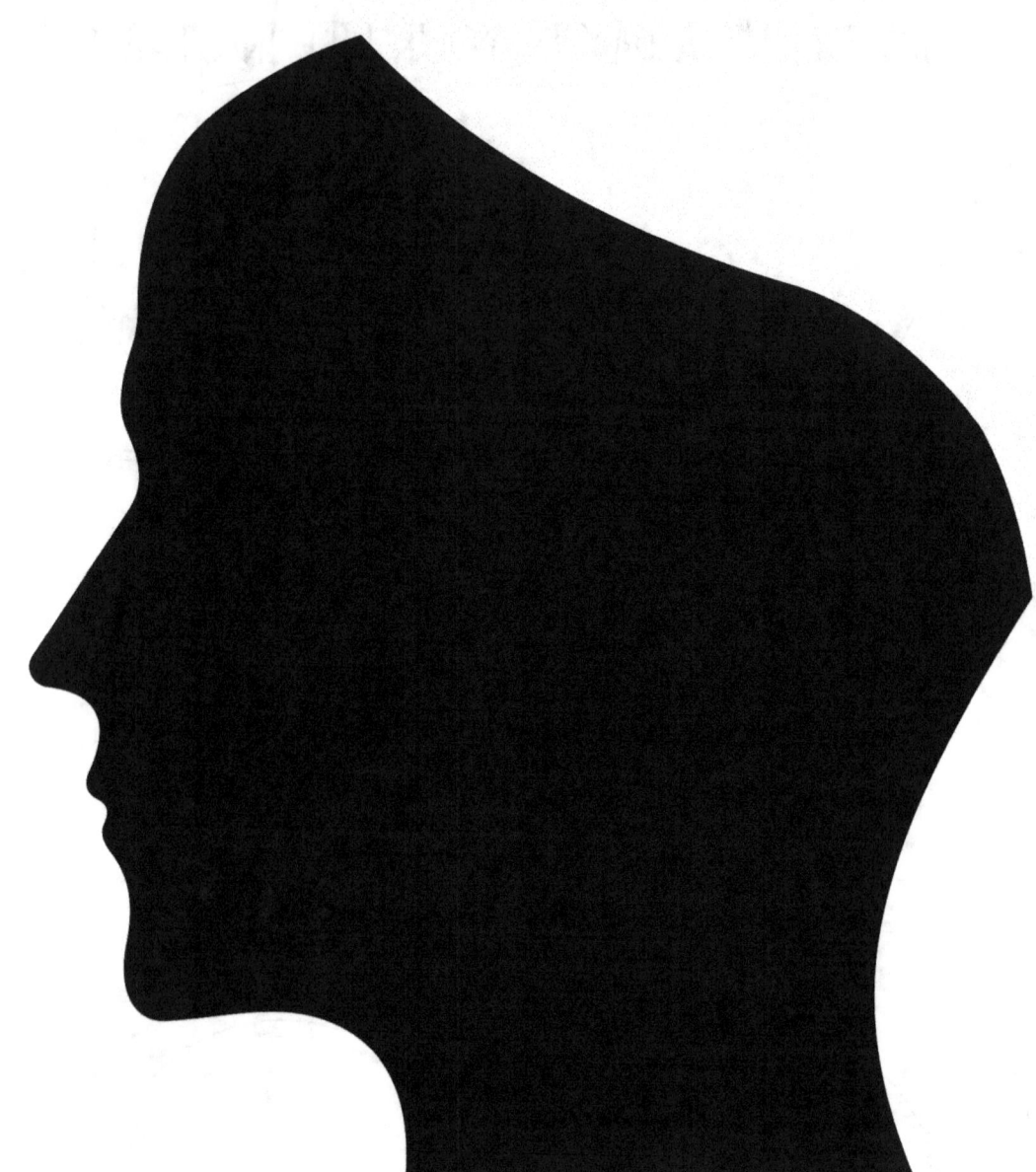

CREATE SOMETHING OUT OF FOLDED PAPER AND FIX IT HERE

SIGNED:
DATE:

WASH DAY
HANG YOUR WASHING OUT TO DRY HERE

SIGNED:
DATE:

WRAP A GIFT
LEAVE IT HERE

SIGNED:
DATE :

SIGNED:
DATE :

CREATE A POP UP SCENE

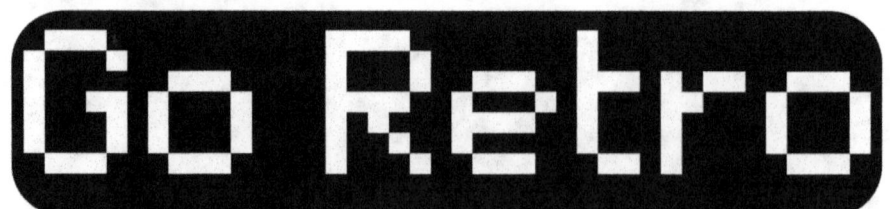

Go retro with some old school nostalgia
and sentimental throwbacks

SIGNED:
DATE :

CREATE A PAGE OF SYMMETRY

SIGNED:
DATE:

CREATE A PAGE OF SYMMETRY

SIGNED:
DATE :

SIGNED:
DATE:

CREATE A PAGE WITHOUT USING YOUR HANDS

SIGNED:
DATE:

EXPERIMENT WITH DIFFERENT TOOLS AND MATERIALS TO CREATE A TEXTURED FEATHER EFFECT

CONNECT . THE . DOTS

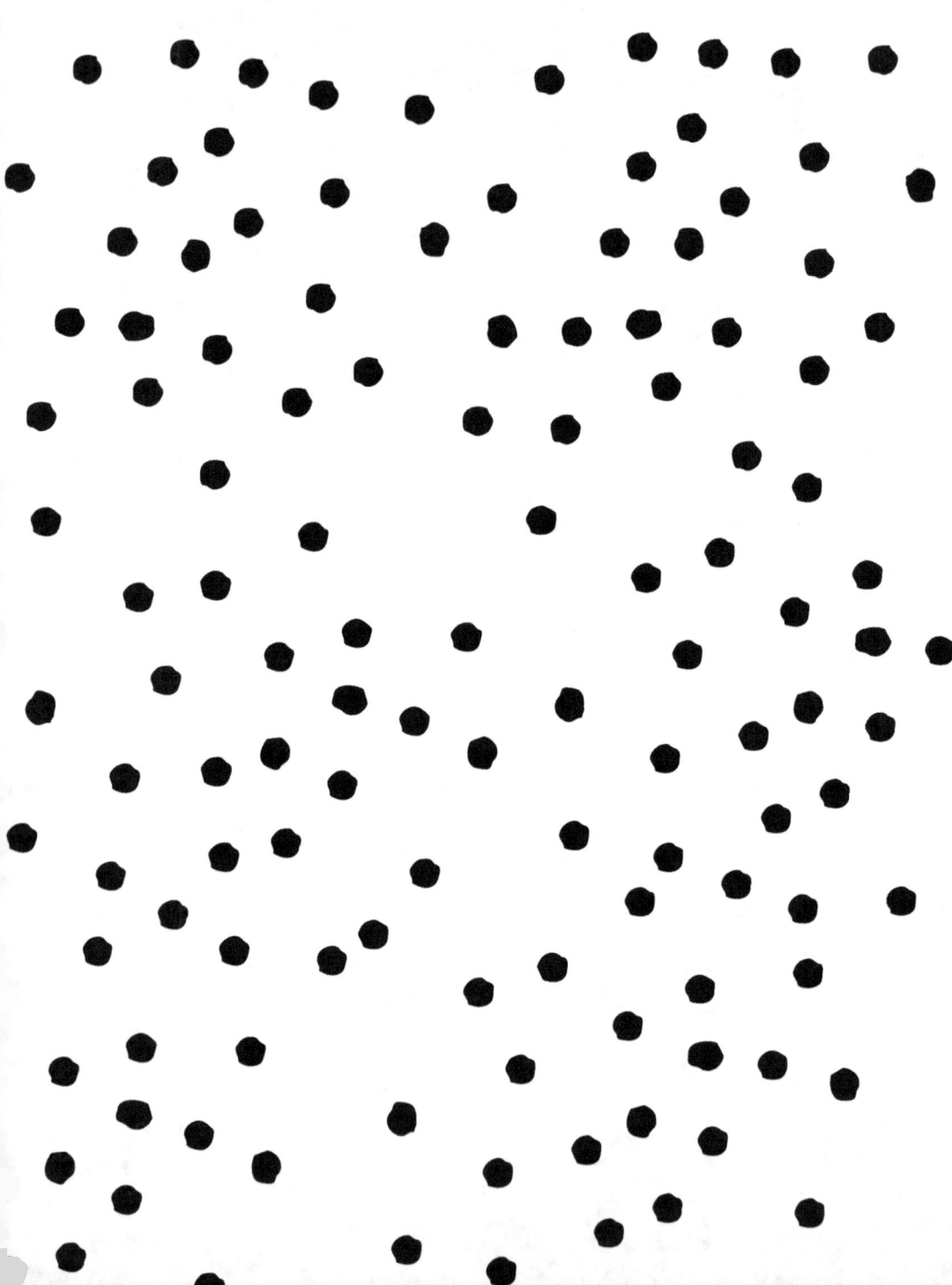

SIGNED:
DATE:

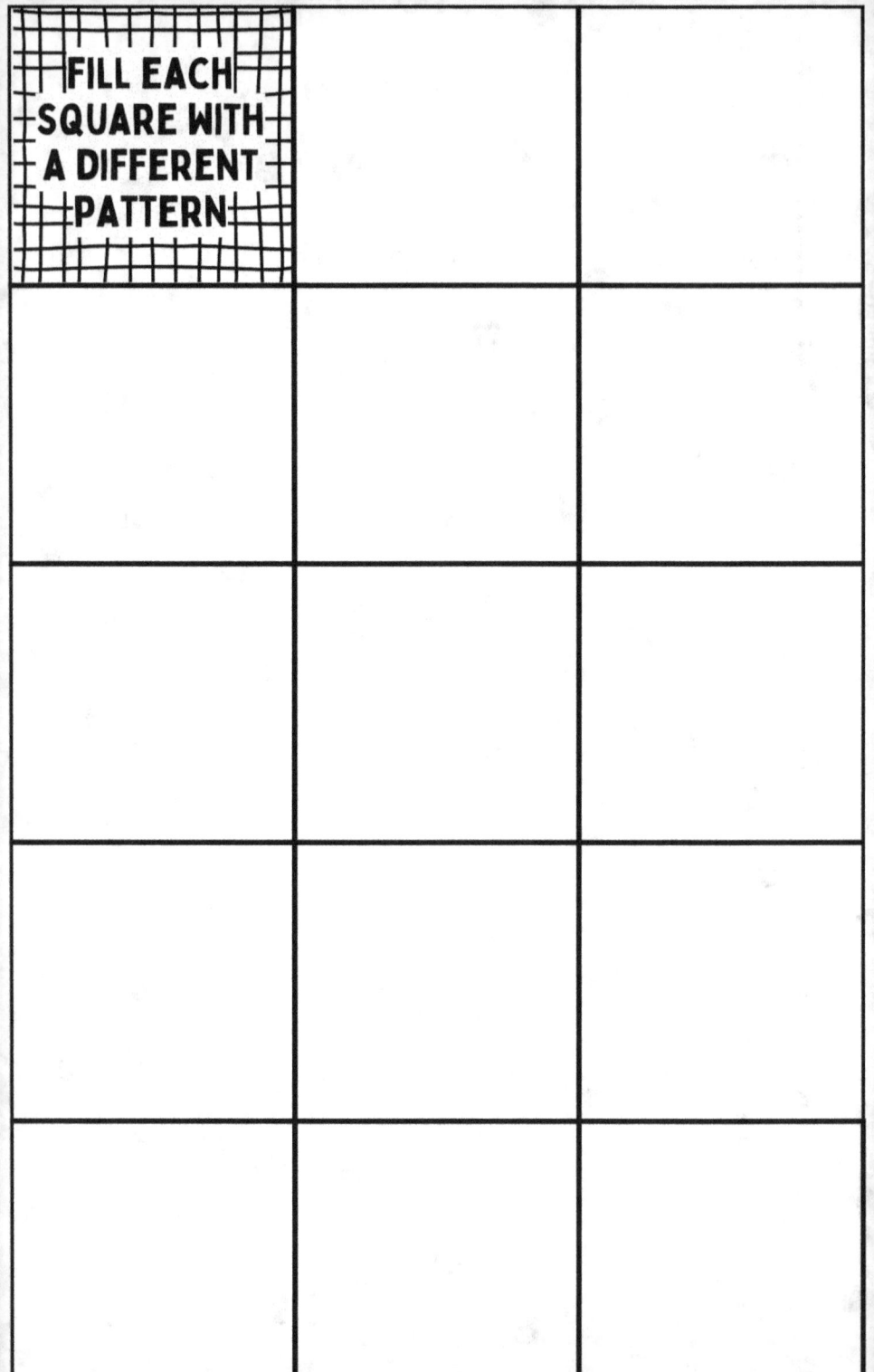

CREATE SOMETHING

HUGE

SIGNED:
DATE :

**CREATE
SOMETHING**
TINY

SIGNED:
DATE :

CREATE TABS TO BOOKMARK YOUR FAV PAGES AND GLUE THEM SO THE TAB IS STICKING OUT OF THE TOP OR SIDE OF THE PAGE.

(APPLY GLUE TO THE SHADED AREA AND STICK THE TAB ON THE REVERSE OF THE PAGE YOU WANT TO MARK)

I LIKE TO STRENGTHEN THE PAPER WITH CARDSTOCK OR CLEAR TAPE.

I LEFT A COUPLE BLANK FOR YOUR OWN LABELS.

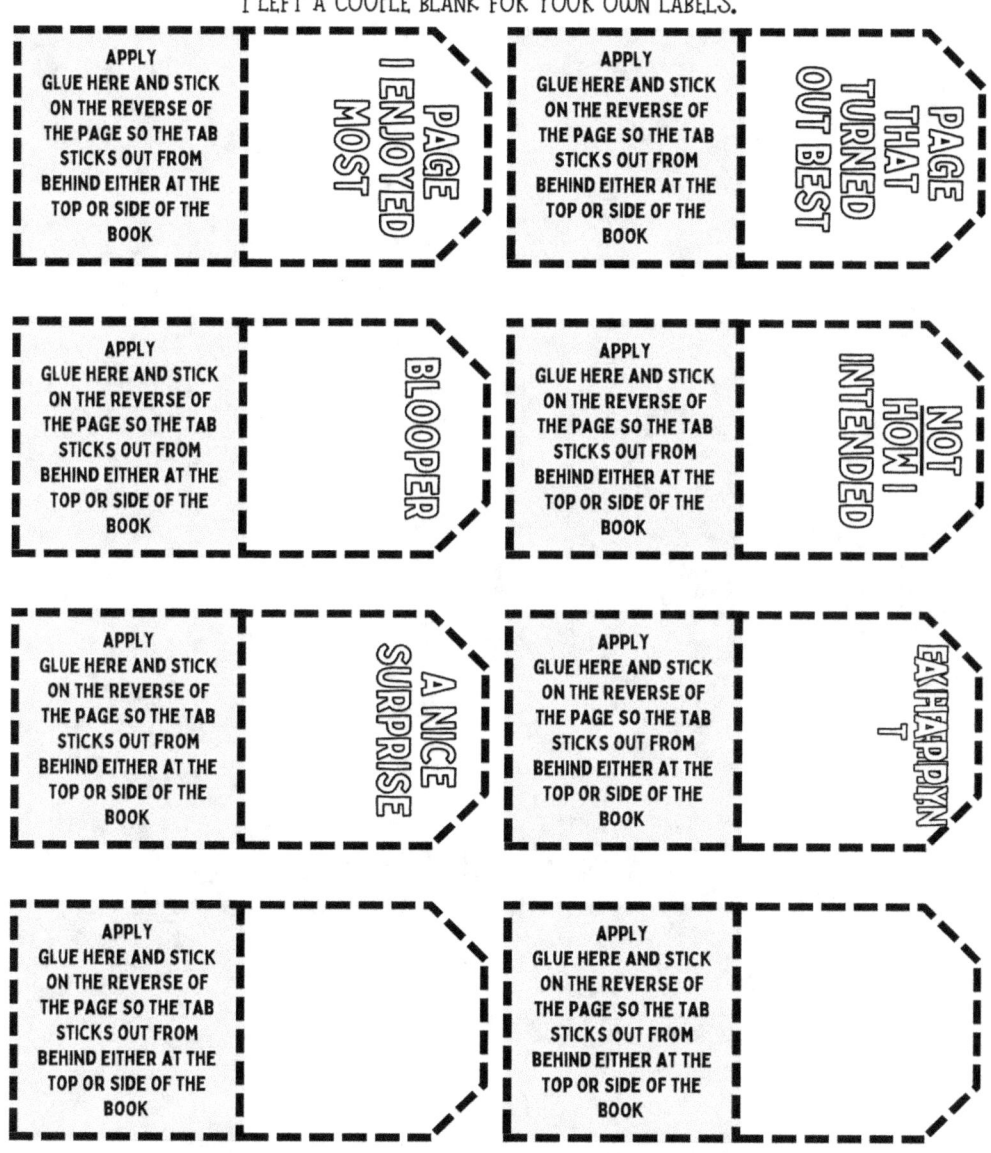

2 BLANK TABS TO ADD YOUR OWN CAPTIONS

| SIGNED: | SIGNED: |
| DATE: | DATE: |

| SIGNED: | SIGNED: |
| DATE: | DATE: |

| SIGNED: | SIGNED: |
| DATE: | DATE: |

| SIGNED: | SIGNED: |
| DATE: | DATE: |

| SIGNED: | SIGNED: |
| DATE: | DATE: |

| SIGNED: | SIGNED: |
| DATE: | DATE: |

| SIGNED: | SIGNED: |
| DATE: | DATE: |

| SIGNED: | SIGNED: |
| DATE: | DATE: |

| SIGNED: | SIGNED: |
| DATE: | DATE: |

| SIGNED: | SIGNED: |
| DATE: | DATE: |

| SIGNED: | SIGNED: |
| DATE: | DATE: |

SPARE PAGE OF LABELS IN CASE YOU NEED TO STICK EXTRA PAGES IN

www.ingramcontent.com/pod-product-compliance
Lightning Source LLC
Chambersburg PA
CBHW072055110526
44590CB00018B/3183